IMPERSONATIONS

MARK ZIMMERMANN

To Charles Walker ⟶

Best wishes,

Mark Zimm⟶

Published by Pebblebrook Press,
an imprint of *Stoneboat*
PO Box 1254
Sheboygan, WI 53082-1254
Editors: Rob Pockat, Signe Jorgenson, Lisa Vihos, Jim Giese
www.stoneboatwi.com

Impersonations ©2015 Mark Zimmermann
LC Control Number: 2015933001
ISBN: 978-0692373019

Printed in the US

Acknowledgments

I thank the editors of the following publications, where the poems below first appeared:

Free Verse: "Emily Dickinson," "Walt Disney," "Thomas Bowdler," "Chidiock Tichborne," "Sei Shōnagon"

The Hartford Avenue Poets anthology *Masquerades and Misdemeanors* (Pebblebrook Press, 2013): "Leni Reifenstahl," "Donald Trump, Sr.," "Dr. Timothy Leary," "Charles Ponzi," "Stefani Germanotta"

New Verse News: "Paul Tibbets," "Willard Mitt Romney"

Stoneboat: "Anna Whistler (Whistler's Mother)," "Mildred Ratched, RN," "Lady Madeline Usher," "Sojourner Truth," "Sigmund Freud"

Vocabula Review: "Victor Frankenstein," "Leonard Zelig," "Col. Robert Ingersoll," "Dr. Jack Kevorkian," "Moby Dick"

Verse Wisconsin: "Anastasia Romanov," "Phineas T. Barnum," "Sir John Falstaff"

Wisconsin Fellowship of Poets Museletter: "Curtis LeMay"

The Writer: "Ted Kaczynski"

Thank you to the following people for help and solidarity along the way: The Hartford Avenue Poets; Lisa Vihos, Signe Jorgenson, Jim Giese, and Rob Pockat at Pebblebrook Press; Phyllis Wax, Mary Lux, and Sheryl Slocum, sharp-eyed proofreaders all; Lewis Turco and Marilyn Taylor, formalists extraordinaire; Marlene Zimmermann, first and best teacher; and Carole Kasprzycki, ever present between the lines and beyond.

Table of Contents

For Carole
first reader, comrade, soulmate

Diana, Princess of Wales

Wine, candles, and a prince are fine
if one prefers fancies or needs an ideal
escape in sleep's care, I was warned.

Wed in flawed fanfare, I soon realised
false appearance is a poison as real
as arsenic in a candied spoon.

I learned a palace lesson as well:
If one is crowned People's Princess, one is
also considered a fool on parade—

scandalised in serial press affairs, fed on
as if a wolf leered in awe of a carcass.
People's Princess indeed, dear reader!

Life spiraled in a world of façade
and I was in. I learned and relied on powers
of appearance in a season of refined warfare.

All is on record. Wine, candles, a prince—
scandal and a final dalliance—all ended
on a wild ride in Paris.

Walt Disney

"A tin wand in a wasteland..."

I see an island, sinless, walled
inside a tall tale. We all need
a tall tale sweet as a twilit sea; I sell
it as a daily aside. All is swell

at Disneyland. We stay inside
it all day—a sandy seaside
den; indeed, we lie in linen
sweetness, see in it a new dawn

daily—lest any sainted
naiads die, salty seas taint
a west wind as we wait, idly,
and any tales ended sadly.

Dr. Timothy Leary

Hey! Let all herald the holy road—
do a hit, meditate,
Hello Earth!

Yeah, I loaded the head.
I dared it to alter
a dead reality.

It did. It relayed
matter to myth-head, related
atom to dreamer.

It married the old order
to mirth armed to the teeth,
yet the old order loathed me.

They'd rather let it all die.
They'd rather adore
the death-head.

Later I did meet Death,
that hardy, mad old hatter.
I made him o.d.!

I died
yet here I am, already
immortal, yeah.

Leonard Zelig

Dora realized an inner no one: I, a loner
in danger, relied on a deadened role—regale
and gladden all near. A lion roared
in a zoo, I roared; an egg roller rolled
a Grade-A egg, I rolled a Grade-A egg.

Did I lie? Or did an eirôn angel zigzag
and linger in ironia no one realized?
Ogling a golden Zelig lode, a zillionaire
regaled Dora and I in doggerel. Agog,
a leaden gang roared: Zelig! Zelig! Zelig!

I ran. Derailed on a red legal line—"Zelig
a Liar!"—I landed a lead role in one deranged
Nazi gala. Dora rode in and I realized:
I need Dora! Again in danger, again
Dora and I ran, rigged a Nazi airliner,

landing on an old line a zillionaire
re-engineered in a golden reading:
"Zelig—No Longer a Liar!"
Did zillionaire gold lie? I ended
realizing an inner longing: Dora.

Anna Whistler (Whistler's Mother)

"Sit still, Mother. Sit still
a moment more. I'm almost there."

Sit still. Sit still, Mother! Oh
how his line is tiresome.

Let me rest awhile, I'm sore.
What's more, the room is too hot.

I stare at the wall.
I want to eat.

When at last mealtime is here
I'll eat a horse!

Well, at least he honors the art.
He tries to see, has wherewithal

to show what is. In this he honors
me as well, a woman who sat,

a mother who wishes
that others will honor her son tomorrow.

I stare at the wall in an ashen room
while I water his art in stillness.

Lady Madeline Usher

Did he say I am dead? Nearly dead? Muddled in serial dreams
he'd assume my demise as I lay ashen, unseen,
my maidenhead a shell in his mind's remains.

He dreams. In shaded denial and misrule he dreams. He is dead
already. His line ends here, in delirium, in red halls realised
as ruin, as nemesis, his and mine.

A hearse's dim and leaden Muse
underlies his need in slurred, unhealed allure.
Undead, I remain a riddle in his madness.

Rev. Arthur Dimmesdale

Let them all see the Devil's truth reveal
a ruthless, ill-starred shimmer that shades
Hester's marauded heart: She lives, reviled,
as I—vested, dulled, mute, ashamed—
am revered as dearest elders are revered.

Ah, there *is* a Devil—ever a liar, a murderer amid tall trees
he lives, mad as all his desires. There did I meet him.
There did I lust. I tasted delirium. I served him.

Shall the elders sever ears that heard the adulterers' tale?
Heal a Salemite that murmured lurid heresies? Sure
as desert trials tested the Israelites, here dread
deviltries ride. As Hester has mastered *her* letter, let all
see it arise—a shield, a veil, a truth reviled!

Grigory Rasputin

Staring into Tsarina's angst, I intuit signs
rising in a rotting gust—traitors rain
tyranny on Russia, our nation a starry ruin!

Praying at an orgy is no sin. O grant us our gorging
on propitiation. Sin is as I say it is
in any situation. Go...go sin, go sin again.

          Atoning,
a patriot gross in sin's torpor, I pray
as utopians turn in array against Russia—

          Rasputin,
trysting satyr...grip upon Tsarina...party
to apostasy...a ranting pagan guru—

            I pray
no assassins gang up to poison Russia!
Sparing no Tsarina, no Tsar, sparing no Rasputin.

Phineas T. Barnum

Here it is!—The Truth in entrepreneur miniature:
I appraise an impure appetite, sate
the masses. Is it a bitter truth? Is pure sunshine
better than sunshine seen in a prism?

I insist it isn't. In this here Supreme Museum
(reprint it in the papers as I narrate), I present
Supreme Triumphs! Empires, ruins, runes!
Truths that bear Nature's human banner—

that banish numbness, temper the brutish;
treasure them here!   See the Siamese brethren sup!
Hear Earth's tiniest heart beat in Mr. Thumb's breast!
At a mere ten pennies per, step up! Step up here!

Willard Mitt Romney

I'm an ordinary millionaire.
I don't need a media elite
to remind me I made money.
Morality demanded I earn
and I did. I made a dream my own.

In my world, one will earn a dollar
or one will want an entitlement.
Indeed, I'd tell any needy, amoral
idler: Don't lean on a millionaire. Learn
to toil—or win ten million in a lottery!

We need a new national order—now—
or we'll all drown in a money drain!
A Ryan-Rand leader, I didn't let
any tweedy elite meddler order me
to reward an addled, idle dream

in Detroit. No—I rallied any and all:
don't wait on an entitlement! I rallied
any and all: earn a real and moral dollar!
I did it and I'm an ordinary man.
I married my dear, dear Ann. We earned
a dollar and made it into a dream.

Charles Ponzi

Hope rose, hope rises, hope shall
channel sales. Rich or poor, people prize
a chance, press in on a real pleaser: I'll enrich all!

*Ponzi? He'll sell a spear carrier a pencil sharpener, sell
a corpse a hearse, an apple a core, Nessie Loch Ness,
an ass a hole!*

Poor cheerless also-rans, I sleep in peace.
Sales rose, sales rise. Cash rolls in
on a peerless plan: Riches, Happiness, Hope!

Donald Trump, Sr.

A small man's monotonous lot
amounts to a rut on a dull map.

A Trump man's dollar amount
maps a natural surplus.

A small man prompts no plan
to add onto unsold land.

A Trump man puts
a dollar amount on all land,

touts an all-out proposal:
Ad Plan   Dollar Plan

Trumpland.
Sold.

Moby Dick

Do Moby Dick?
I'd dock my id, kid.

Mock Moby Dick—"O Moby,
O cod mommy"—mock
doom, yo!

OK'd by moody dick,
odd mob did do my bod.
I KO'd my odd, moody mob.

My bio OK'd doom:
Oy, I'm Moby Dick!

Bartleby, Scrivener

Certain last letters
are earnestly sent
yet never arrive.

Restive strivers
vainly translate
nil, vastness.

An alternative:
rebel
in silence.

I believe
in silence
as it settles

in a lantern never lit,
in a letter vainly sent,
carnal silence

irresistibly severe,
intractable,
senseless.

Eternities
incarcerate all.
I starve.

I stare.

Thomas Bowdler

Too lewd to allow, the Bard's words retard
morals. We assessed, we rewrote: *bastard*
shall read as *lad; the bawd* as *the Mrs.*
All to theatre's better health.   Alas,

there's more low drama. Base mortals howl, swear
mad oaths to the world—Hamlet, Othello, Lear—
what a drear morale to tower, morose,
a threat to lad or lass. Amoral bard, whose

desolate words debase readers' health.
Worlds blow as hot dream—what wasted breath!
What a waster's maw! Well we assessed the lot.
Abashed, we deleted or rewrote the rot.

Marquis de Sade

I require maids' dear asses
sure as muses
require dreamers. Read me

as I ream said ass. Queer
ideas arise; I am deemed mad.
Rum reader, squirm—

I squire reamed asses!
as demure maids assure
us: Sadism's sum

is a rare red masque,
a murdered seed,
a muse's dead requiem.

Ed Gein

Dig I did
indeed.
Digging ended,
I edged in

edged in
need.

I needed,
I dined.
Dining ended,
I die.

Sigmund Freud

Greed, murder, mind under fire—
disfigured urges
ensure suffering.

If murder is deified,
suffering drummed in,
surrender ensues.

Energies dim, find refuge
in sin's medium:
feminine desire.

Suffering endures. Mmm...

If I refigure mind,
if in refiguring duress
I undermine sin—sin dies,

demiurges die, deified
ruses die—I'd free
minds under siege.

If...if indeed!
Suffering endures.
Mind under fire.

Four Horsemen

Some foresee
one foe's house
of omen, no rune
or ruse more sour.

Here no Ur-men
or horses run
offshore. Here
men run for home:

seers, he-men,
sufferers—
our men of furor,
men of more hours.

Leni Riefenstahl

At the rallies he shines.
His rites instill
in all the fatherless
an inner star, a fire, the faith.

An aesthete, I relate it
in Arian art: *Heil Hitler!*

If there is fire
all I see
as an artist
is fire.

Heinrich Himmler

Ein Himmel,
ein Reich; immer
ein Reich im Himmel,
ein heiler Himmel—
Heil!

I cheer. I cheer
Him. I cheer Him
here.   In Hell
I'll cheer henchmen,
crime, ice.

Note: The first stanza translates as "One sky,/one Reich; always/a Reich in the sky,/a holy sky—/Heil!"

Paul Tibbets

It appalls—as bullets appall.
Battle built it;
labs test it,
label it: U.S.A.

I use it.
Plate, bat, ball:
a blast leaps.

Put up a slate tablet? Salute
Paul Tibbets? Bull.
Let all applause pass. I'll sleep—
a late, pale blip.

Curtis LeMay

Lame terms create a malaise—useless
truces, airy treaties, arms limits—eyeless terms all
easily met as Russia cruelly rules
all it masters: easterly states, small
martyr satellites. I say, Resist!

Let me state my terms clearly:
A limitless aerial assault'll cure
a crummy malaise, cream Russia. Let's use it!
My SAC missiles'll melt all Russia's cities,
mister. I'll slay Russia.

America's cities? As all arms races are ties
(a sissy ruse), Russia'll maul us as a result?
Let it try! Cities are trail meat. America
must resist Russia, assault Russia, slay it!

Toge Sankichi

"Chichi o kaese haha o kaese
...ningen o kaese"

At night I see the giant
skinning his ghost in a cage.
Oka-san sickens. She chokes,
is gone, is gone. I kiss
oka-san, see no one.

At night I see an ankh
hanging, hot on the giant's chain.
Oka-san, the chain is tightening,
snakeskin in a knot.   I choke.
                Oka-san, I see nothing.

Tonight a kite in the gingko
ate the stinging ant.
Oka-san, the snake in the gingko
ate the kite's one kin. Is that,
oka-san, the no one I see?

Note: The epigraph is a transliterated excerpt from "Prelude," Toge's
poem on the atomic bombings of Nagasaki and his hometown,
Hiroshima. The epigraph translates as "Bring back father bring back
mother/...bring back humanity"

Lafcadio Hearn

Loner on a life errand,
in far-off Nihon I call
on a land of odd lore.

And if here
      I find one fair daffodil, a relic-laden
      alien coffer, or one circle coaled
      on an olden calendar, ah,

I'll color
      and herald arcane difference. For in old Nihon
      elder dead lie in hand—cache of riffled hair
      on a far hill, an old hill—

and here, alone
      in a corner, an elfin child feared
      a rice doll and cried. A far-off dolor echoed
      in her call: *Here I once had a life.*

Sei Shōnagon

I.
Henna, sage, sea-shine.
An inn sign hangs—see
again he is gone.

II.
One has a song, one
has an ego high in song—
I see a sign, ash.

III.
In singing again
I sigh. As ages go so
ages shine, asea.

Dr. Jack Kevorkian

Even in vain, care;
do a kind deed. Never in vain
did one care and die—

a dare in a koan vein. I arrive
in dire and drained accord—
door near, creed ajar
and I never revive a one.

Do a kind deed—odd nerve
reckoned in a driven voice:
I did care. I do care. I do.

Ted Kaczynski

I can't stand it. A dazed intensity kicks in:
statistics can a dynastic state dank
and inane in stasis. Days, days, decades…

desk-addicted cases kiss decadent ass
as I edit a candid cease-and-desist attack
and send it in.

Did any die?
Can a decadent statistic die?
A staid and sickened NYT can't edit destiny!

Gregor Samsa

Gore me,
see me roam agog—
a room smearer
gross as orgasm.

Mildred Ratched, RN

A talented criminal, he came
in decline and riled the men, created
ill attachment in a card dealer act,
then cheated them all.

He'll need critical care. He'll need
medicine. Let him remain
here in treatment.
I'll handle him.

I mean it. Earlier, medicine had calmed
all the men here; in time it'll calm him.
Add the electrical treatment
and I am certain:

In the end he'll relent
and attain mental health.

Hannibal Lecter, MD

Here at table, Clarice—a delectable
table indeed, dear Clarice—in calm manner rebel,
learn the thrill. Embrace the dare and let it all ride
till birth and death meet in the dirt.

Clarice, dear Clarice, let me retell an ancient tale:
A man ate three mice. Later he learned
that three blind men lamented the dead mice.
Then the man danced
and bled and ate the three blind men.

Dear, dear Clarice, let it be recalled:
A mere dilettante can eat a dead animal.
A mere madman can eat a man-brain.
I eat the dead mind and attain internal balance.

Winston Smith

Months on
it's not too soon
to show who I'm into.

I motion
to Him.

His mission
is to shit
on Winston Smith.

I'm so into Him.
I'm His minion

on show,
soon shot.
Winston Smith.

Now I'm His. Now
I'm not.

Osama bin Laden

Islam is all.
Man is made
in Islam.

And as man
is old as sand, so
Islam is oasis.

One denies
Islam, one is
dead—

dead, one loses
all. Loses all
and is damned.

The Whore of Babylon

Lo! The Whore of Babylon wrote
a letter to Abby,
who'll foretell all:

Hey honey, blow no wolf
on the altar of a boor; he'll not be
thy baby, he'll be all woof!
Let thy rebel heart yell,
robe off—the yellow eye
of a real whore'll fall on thy halter.
Let that fool only eye thy booty!
For baby, of boor beware:
A hater of all Babylon he be,
he of yore who wrote, "the whore..."

Benito Mussolini ("Il Duce")

See, no doubt is touted. No mind's dimmed
in delusion! One bum bolts,
one muted bum obit. Not one ill mote
is to soil men's lot, intense toil.

To be on time men must toil
in unison, see? I, too, must be
on time so I bless one tune
till silent men in line boom out.
                In sum, I unite!

One timeline, I'll be its tenet!
Unless cold bombs blot us out,
bet no less. Time to mull
bootless tombs is not mine.

Thich Quang Duc

Hiding in a ditch at night
an ant can dig in, haunt a giant
and gain that ditch.

Chanting—again again again—
a dug-in night ant can taunt,
unhinging a giant.

I didn't dig, didn't taunt, didn't
quit.
      I act.

Lt. William "Rusty" Calley

Always a steamy misery—lice eat
at will, crawlers claw. Trees eye us.

A rural area seems clear, a little later
rice-eater trails are a tracer-lit mire.

Casualties rise.
Weary, we curse war.

We curse all its cruelty. We curse
trees—trees are scum lairs.

At trial I see career lawyers at war;
my accusers tar me as lawless, cruel.

True, I was careless at My Lai.
I rue my acts.

Yet, were my acts crimes? I recall
a U.S. air war calculus: *Waste 'em all.*

I rue my acts.
I rest my case.

Ernesto "Che" Guevara

No one staggers our honor here.
Our guns are to vacuous
northern rot as hunters' gunshots
are to the target.

Strength to avenge our heroes,
courage to secure Havana. No gun?
Then heave a stone!

Our hearts, greater than stones
or guns, chart a course
to true honor, to revere correct strength,
to govern truth. Truth runs the street.

Anastasia Romanov

I sit in a room,
transom vista: rain
or moon or stars or
mist, no visitation.

So?   It is not in vain.
I am a Romanov.

Rainstorm in a samovar,
rats on a minor moon—
assassins storm in. I soar
into vast air.

Emily Dickinson

Men needed me, keen
on lily meekness. So do I nod
in my domed mode—on skin's isle
kinsmen line my dolmen.

Kiss, men—kiss
my likeness—lonely skill.
In domes I see demimonde
men's old eyes.

So cold—dimity men—coolly
demised. Domed
I line my Eminence, Deo.

Sir John Falstaff

Of Honor, Hal, or of its joint fashions,
tho' fair strains of Honor soon join
a toast to hail fair traits, alas,
if "Honor" stirs fools to toil in rash fits
all's aslant.
If all's aslant, Honor, too, is aslant.

Honor?   I'll toast Honor, Hal!
To Honor—a star on a fool's hairshirt!
To Honor—hoarfrost final on a harlot's tit!
To Honor—halo of a rash on a lion's ass!
That is all of it, Hal. I insist that is all. So
all hail Honor as I honor a fair lass's loins...

To a fair lass's loins!
Hal?   Hal?

Victor Frankenstein

In a test of secret invention, I revere
infinities, increase of fact, reason.
Ancient certainties face a transient frontier;
reserve no encore!   In science's version
of creation, a fakir or far off seer
invents arcana, stories, incarnates
fear of skies, fire, seas, ice. A savior
arrives: renaissance visions of science
free a creator to fear no constraint
in arc or force of invention. I foresee
rock for a stone-carver ever constant
in narration of necro-artistries.

As Victor's freak, I...I savor no kiss.
Cast off, afire, I sink in seas of ice.

Chidiock Tichborne

One credo the robed decider intoned:
I die. No choir to reckon the end note—
the cock cried. I do not die in bed.
Be there no tender other to rend
the dire cord? Neck to be broken
I brood on the deed, cornered. No door
here be tried. Do I end hidden?
To be born or not, to die knotted or
borne on one thin note cried
to beck the end: I be not broken.
Tick-tock, tick-tock. I die
not in terror. The Tichborne
end be not one to think bitter on.
I die here encoded in the eon.

Col. Robert Ingersoll

Clerics' reigns gorge on stolen liberties.
Clerics reign too long—robbing, bringing
"signs," or telling stories to terrorise
gentle beings till inner liberties
be lost in bingeing on Cross gore. Sensing
rot, I ring no bell to clerics. I greet
clerics: go ring bells, go in clerics' robes, tell
Bible stories clerics tell.   Still—
since no cleric longs to toil in silence, let
no belligerent cleric silence one
stoic, libertine, or sirens' choir.
Belonging to no sect,
I ignore stillborn "eternities,"
bring cool sense to belie.

Mary Mallon (Typhoid Mary)

Maid in N.Y. Typhoid Drama!
Mary Mallon: Plainly a Mad Liar!
It all ran to paranoia.

I am no Pandora, dammit.
And I am no party to typhoid.
I am not ill!

Prior to all that daily rot in print
I'd play my tiny part, mind
my lot.

Today I rot
in a dayroom, party
to no pain or any harm.

I'll not play martyr
to all that primal
paranoia,

dammit!

Marina Oswald Porter

Was it all an international plot
or was Lee in it alone?
Someone in power
possesses real answers.
I don't.

I married a man,
not an assassin.
Still, to dwell on it
and remain a widow
was a waste.

I made a new start,
remarried, resettled.

I'm an old woman now.
Let it alone.

Judas Iscariot

As I said, trust
is a start. Ajar
to riot's court

distrust is a door
to sour accord. So
I rot, I roar: *I did it!*

Distrust is art, too—
a crass art,
its Cross torrid.

Jay Silverheels (Tonto)

It's television,
not history.
I'll say that.

I'll also say
that a lone hero
isn't trivial.

This one's
a visionary.
He lives

not only to rove
or as a saint on a horse—
he yearns to save lives

that no one'll ever save,
all the stolen lives that join
the holes I see in his eyes,

the holes
I see
in leather.

History has its heroes,
television its tales.
Neither'll vanish, ever...

Hi-yo Silver!

Thomas Kinkade

As an antidote to the assessment
Kinkade has no taste, I detest him!
I'd add: This idea doesn't
diminish me. Instead I think
on Him. Moment to moment
I stand in testament to Him,

testament in His shades. And I thank
Him as His immense Dominion shines,
shines in skies He made. And as He made
the skies, He made Man. And as He made
Man, He made Man a home. Isn't
that a testament to His kindness?

So I am not ashamed to admit
I attend to His Domain. And sometimes
in the end those that damn me aid Him,
hasten some to take His side, as in *Detest*
Kinkade? That's the same as to detest Him
and His immense Domain—No thanks!

As to the demeaned estimate that I am
the nation's most in-demand aesthete—
I am! (And I amass the most assets, too.)
This is no stain on me! I tithe and aid
those in need—in His name. The name
that shines in the tiniest home.

And as He dominates the moment, I see
Him, ease into His name's sake,
thank Him, and am His. Indeed I am His.

John Wayne (Marion Morrison)

Men's mission on Iwo Jima—
win honor in war.

My mission was easier—
win WWII on a horse.

Men on Iwo Jima were heroes,
men in arms, warriors who shone.

As I enjoy heroism's sheen
a *Why* remains.

Why in a way I am no hero.
Why in a way I am.

Thomas Pynchon

Amass too many phantoms,
Ms. Maas? Any postman can co-opt
a catch-as-catch-can psy-op scam;
many a map, too many phony stamps
attach to a po-mo cosmos.
So, Ms. Maas, ha-ha's amp
a sop to a chatty spy, yo! Can psycho
phantoms man my topos, not co-opt
a mass, pay-at-any-cost past?

P.S. No photos.

Baby Jane Hudson

Does Daddy say Jane's a has-been?
Oh shush—Daddy says Jane's No.1!

Does Daddy say Jane's been bad?
Oh no—Daddy says Jane's dandy!

Does Daddy say Jane's sane?
Oh yes, Daddy says so. He does!

Does a jaded nobody say
"Jane, Jane, Jane, Daddy's dead"?

Yes! Yes!—a jaded nobody,
jaded nobody! Oh Daddy, Daddy...

Daddy, Jane, sand and sea
on a sunny, sunny Baby Jane day!

Stefani Germanotta

Fame enters me as I sing,
stoning me in figments of image. Agog
I offer finger treats to monsters.
Go on, stare at me!

Onstage, fame is an intimate engagement;
fans are a star's greatest gift, a mirror
of sorts. Into it I sing for Roman orgies
as monsters gorge on a feast of frottage.

Get off on it, man!
I am a meat-eater rising
to trigger stranger fantasies. As for fame,
it, too, rises onstage.

I taste it.
I stagger offstage.
I am Gaga!

Manfred von Richthofen

Victor and victim are made of each other.
In their mid-air death match
honor and horror are one.

I dove in on him. He tried to veer off.
     I fired, he died.
He'd have fired, too,
if he'd had the chance.

On terra firma have faith in mechanic.
In the air have faith in machine.
Did I mention that here and there I fear death?

Did it matter that I dreamed a red omen
in thin air? Fate had no foreordained
favorite there. Neither did I—
never overrate or demean a foe.

Elizabeth Cady Stanton

As to destiny, ancient and hazy notions
easily attach to childhood lessons:
the Bible says this,
the Bible says that.

In Eden she ate sin, instilled
it in all, instilled death in all
and since then
no one conscience is clean
so abide by the holy lesson
else blaze in Hell!

Oh, is that all?
It's all on the lady?
In this lesson, so-called,
nonsensical
ideas, haloed as holy,
shine on.

A lady, Bathsheba's descendant, stood
tallest—the one chosen
chaste and sinless as the Son she had,
she has a destiny identical
to His: Deathless they ascend.

Ladies, I elect to not stand
in these idealized shades!
I'll not only state this,
I'll teach it, stand by it,
debate anyone on it.

Thomas Friedman

Tom Friedman here, Times Minister
of Free Trade and Fresh Ideas,
a neo-astronomer
resident this moment on Mars.

And as I ride the Martian metro, I meet
a Martian rider, a Martian tradesman
transformed on the Marsnet, for he mines
free data on the Earthman Adam Smith

in his metro rider free time, shares
that information, sends
it to other Martians on the Marsnet,
and transforms Martian trade. I am the first

to note that he is an Adamite hero!
And in an instant I see
that he defines ordinariness, that
ordinariness is his main asset.

It means he is a trendsetter.
It means he is an insider.
Soon I define his mind as *Martian;*
at the same time I define him.

This doesn't mean that Mars
or the ordinariness of its tradesmen
interest me one Martian iota.
Faith in free trade—there's the idea!

Indeed, I insist on it as the one road
to a neo-Martian transformation.
As the Times Minister of Free Trade
and its resident seer (I see stars)

I therefore mean to address
the nations of Earth and Mars: I foresee
a mass, free tradesman, Marsnet trend
hot on the neo-Martian frontier!

Charles Augustus Lindbergh

As Israelites aren't Arians
and Chinese aren't Caucasians,
as genes and racial lineage
endure in a natural alliance
that sets the standard regarding
cultural hierarchies, it stands
that genetics and eugenics
are essential in understanding
and arranging such hierarchies.

Engineering acts here as a decider.
The engineer addresses an issue, situates
and scales it, then, sure as Nature selects
genes that succeed, he creates
a design, tests it, and acts.
Designs that endure
the harshest testing result in success
(as in trans-Atlantic engine design).
Designs at less than grade are discarded.
Let us all salute the engineers.

Eugenics and engineering are related
in the sense that each addresses
distinct natures and crucial issues.
The issues are: genetic inheritance,
racial status, miscegenetic threats;
and instituting genetic, racial, and cultural
standards that ensure health in all races,
that target and cure the deadliest ills
endangering this Earth. Here in the 1930s

the Third Reich has instituted such standards.
Indeed, as I see it Hitler is a great leader.
Standing against this and race-related truths,
Churchill and his Israelite gang set
a radical agenda: tilt the scales, agitate
against the Reich, against the U.S.A.'s
neutral stance in this decade's titanic crisis.
Shall such an alliance dictate U.S. interests?
As I said earlier, understanding
racial hierarchies is essential.

Granted, races and cultures aren't diseases.
And as racial hatred denigrates
hater and hated, it scales at less than grade.
Still, eugenics and genetics are necessities,
as are the racial allegiances
that Nature has engineered,
that cultural inheritance illustrates,
that the engineer and eugenicist each desire.
This isn't racial hatred—it is a higher truth!

Greatrakes the Stroker (Valentine Greatrakes)

As lightning shakes a tree on a hill, singeing
tho' not killing its leaves, so I liken Heaven striking
to a stark, torrential revelation: *Greatrakes, listen!*—

Neither startle to this aghast nor let it astonish.
In England the King's Evil levies a toll severe
so take to the healer's art, travel
to those lingering in travail—even
the loneliest sinner, one else lost
ghosting in Hell smoke—then, in vigor attentive
restore health. In this as in all things
think not as a savior. Heal as a servant.

O, I give thanks to His eternal love! Tho' it is not original
to Earth, neither is it set as a starling egg
in a stranger's nest, ever alien.
No, no—sharing eternal love I stroke rotting sores
till into the skies the King's Evil vanishes.
Then I give thanks, again, again, again.

Mrs. Anne Gilchrist

As I see in that last letter, the man
singing in earlier lines
isn't, in a literal sense, real.

The man in that letter, he isn't
the great man in the grass,
a message that hit me as strange.

Still, the timeless images—his
grass, his night, in his calm manliness
a testament that all is eternal—

these are electric streams that attract
all higher sentiment.
In this I see greatness.

In a similar sense, the lesser men's images—
aghast in critical cant—aren't real,
grate in missing larger interest:

ancient instinct, Earth as altar, as Grail;
the sacral scent animating Man,
the great artist's greeting.

Then let me relate it here, again:
all earlier allegiance remains
intact, literal, timeless.

Meantime, tell me. Tell all.
Is the "real man" there
in that last letter sent?

Sincerest in heart
I remain,

Anne

Sojourner Truth

—Juneteenth's ours!

The South touts honor, trust,
truth to her sons.
To us? Noth'n.

The South's one unjust
house! Noth'n to us, noth'n
to honor or trust.

Southern house
unjust house—
Here's the stone truth—

Sojourner, she's not returnin'.
The route's north—
the route's out!

The Elvis Impersonator

Some Elvis lovers have never seen
the real man live. As I morph
to please them, I repeat
the one mantra: *I am not a solo artist—*
Elvis is here in the room!

The Elvis elite remain hostile.
To them I'm a mere impostor,
a satellite in thrall to Planet Elvis,
no more than a noteless parasite.
That I serve the man means little to them.

Perhaps it is all a matter of taste.
Thespians live on imitation;
portrait painters interpret lives.
These impersonators thrive
on their status as artistes.

Other times I sense
the elites have a point—
that I am at most an impostor
similar to insane prisoners
most alive in other selves.

Here at the Elvis shrine in Memphis
it's time I sent the elite a response.
As soon as tonite's revue starts,
I'll morph to the mantra:
Elvis is here in the room!

Yeti (Abominable Snowman)

I am an animal, yes,
not a wanton so bent
by animosities as to slay
men at any moment,
not an enemy to be
blown away at will.

Absent yet able to listen in
on Man, I witness
a bestial monotony:
nations battle, slay
millions, blame enemies,
toll a blameless bell.

Well, Man *is* an animal,
in some ways noble, too.
May my intention to see
Man only as Man *is*
not be a lonely, total waste.
We'll see. Yes, we'll see.

A Note on Form

All of the poems in this book are lipograms, a literary form whereby one or more letters of the alphabet are deliberately excluded from a work. In the case of the poems here, the formal constraint is determined by using only letters appearing in the name of a poem's title subject. For example, all words in "Moby Dick" contain only letters drawn from the letter pool i-o-b-c-d-k-m-y; all words in "Grigory Rasputin" use only letters from the pool a-i-o-u-g-n-p-r-s-t-y, and so forth. The vast majority of the poems in this collection use less than half the letters of the alphabet.

Author Bio

Mark Zimmermann is a Wisconsin native and holds degrees in English from the University of Wisconsin-Milwaukee. Between 1990 and 2004, he lived in Japan, the Netherlands, Hungary, and Poland, where he worked as a university instructor and freelance journalist/editor. As a second and third language user during those years abroad, he experienced linguistic limitations similar to the lipogram's constraints. He feels that this experience is responsible for a good part of his attraction to the form. Since his return to the United States, he has taught humanities and writing courses at the Milwaukee School of Engineering, where he received the Johnson Controls Award for Teaching Excellence in 2013. He is also a member of the Hartford Avenue Poets and represents the Wisconsin Fellowship of Poets on the Wisconsin Poet Laureate Commission. His poetry has appeared in numerous journals and in the anthology *Masquerades and Misdemeanors* (Pebblebrook Press, 2013). Zimmermann lives in Milwaukee with his wife and two cats.